WORKBOOK FOR AFTER THE RAPTURE

A practical guide to David Jeremiah's Book

An End Times Guide To Survival

KPC PUBLISHERS

Copyright © 2023 KPC PUBLISHERS

information on the topics covered and should not be

workbook, whether through electronic or mechanical

The content of this workbook is protected by copyright.

means, including photocopying, recording, or any

If you require expert assistance, it is recommended that

Reproduction or transmission of any part of this

information storage and retrieval system, is prohibited

without written permission from the copyright owner.

considered as a substitute for professional or legal advice.

This workbook is intended to provide general you seek the services of a qualified professional.

Table Of Contents

HOW TO USE THIS WORKBOOK

PART ONE

CHAPTER SUMMARY 1: UNVEILING THE BIBLICAL FOUNDATIONS OF THE RAPTURE

KEY LESSONS

SELF REFLECTION QUESTIONS

LIFE CHANGING ACTIVITIES

CHAPTER SUMMARY 2: VEILED PROPHECIES

KEY LESSONS

SELF REFLECTION QUESTIONS

LIFE CHANGING ACTIVITIES

CHAPTER SUMMARY 3: THE UNVEILING OF ETERNITY

Key lesson

SELF REFLECTION QUESTIONS

LIFE CHANGING ACTIVITIES

CHAPTER SUMMARY 4: EMBRACING HOPE AMIDST CHAOS
KEY LESSONS
SELF REFLECTION QUESTIONS
LIFE CHANGING ACTIVITIES
PART TWO
CHAPTER SUMMARY 5: SIGNS AND PROPHECIES
KEY LESSONS
SELF REFLECTION QUESTIONS
LIFE CHANGING ACTIVITIES
CHAPTER SUMMARY 6: THE LIFELINE OF LOVE
KEY LESSONS
SELF REFLECTION QUESTIONS
LIFE changing activities
CHAPTER SUMMARY 7: NAVIGATING THE END-TIMES MAZE
KEY LESSONS
SELF REFLECTION QUESTIONS

LIFE CHANGING ACTIVITIES
CHAPTER SUMMARY 8: FINDING SOLACE IN SCRIPTURE
KEY LESSONS
SELF REFLECTION QUESTIONS
LIFE CHANGING ACTIVITIES
CHAPTER SUMMARY 9: NAVIGATING RELATIONSHIPS IN A TRANSFORMED WORLD
KEY LESSONS
SELF REFLECTION QUESTIONS
LIFE CHANGING ACTIVITIES

WORBOOK FOR AFTER THE RAPTURE

A practical guide to David Jeremiah's Book

AN END TIMES GUIDE TO SURVIVAL

KPC PUBLISHERS

HOW TO USE THIS WORKBOOK

brief overview of the main points and ideas presented in

These exercises are designed to help you integrate the

Complete the Life Changing Exercises for each chapter.

each chapter from the main book. This will give you a

the original text.

Next, review the Key Lessons section for each chapter.

workbook, or to set aside time to work on them

making positive changes. You may find it helpful to

To use the workbook, begin by reading the summary of

understanding of the main book.

complete these exercises as you work through the

material into your daily life, and to take action towards
help you think critically about the material, and to apply
question carefully, and write down your thoughts and
Once you are through with the workbook, use the
This section will highlight the most important takeaways
After reviewing the Key Lessons, move on to the Self
it to your own life. Take your time to consider each
answers in the space provided for that.
from the chapter, and provide you with a deeper
Reflection Questions. These questions are designed to
separately.
Personal Notes section to record your thoughts, reflections, and insights. This section is for your own
progress and growth over time.

can gain a deeper understanding of the material and make
Generally, the workbook is designed to be a
By working through each chapter, completing the
personal use, and can be a valuable tool for tracking your
comprehensive and interactive guide to the main book.
exercises, and reflecting on your own experiences, you
positive changes in your life.

PART ONE

CHAPTER SUMMARY 1: UNVEILING THE BIBLICAL FOUNDATIONS OF THE RAPTURE

As we dig into the embroidery of End-Times prediction, the idea of the Satisfaction arises as an enamoring and confounding string. Its foundations stretch profound into the pages of the Holy book, winding around a story that sparkles interest and thought.

The excursion starts in the old texts of the Hebrew Scripture, where traces of a heavenly social occasion are dispersed like unlikely treasures. The prophet Isaiah, in his dreams, discusses when the steadfast will be lifted from the earth, getting away from the looming judgment. Daniel's predictions likewise reverberation this subject, anticipating a restoration of the honest.

Notwithstanding, it is in the New Confirmation that the idea of the Bliss turns out to be more unequivocal. The Witness Paul, in his letters to the Thessalonians and Corinthians, reveals the secret of this groundbreaking occasion. He portrays a second when devotees will be up to speed in the mists to meet the Ruler in the air, a second that rises above the limits of natural presence.

The Good news of Matthew further adds to the groundwork of the Bliss, with Jesus himself suggesting a partition between the exemplary and the corrupt toward the finish of the age. The illustrations of the wheat and the tares, the insightful and silly virgins, portray a heavenly arranging, where the dedicated are recognized and assumed to a position of security.

The multifaceted embroidery acquires intricacy as the Messenger John, in the Book of Disclosure, offers looks at heavenly scenes where hoards from each country stand before the privileged position, dressed in white robes. Could this be the climax of the Delight, a great gathering of the recovered?

As we piece together these scriptural parts, the idea of the Euphoria arises not as a simple religious hypothesis but rather as an agreeable tune reverberating through the Sacred writings. It is a crescendo, working from the murmurs of the prophets to the express lessons of Christ and the missionaries.

In our mission to comprehend the complexities of End-Times prescience, unwinding the secret of the Delight turns into a crucial section. A section coaxes us to investigate the significant associations between the Old and New Confirmations, welcoming us to ponder the heavenly arrangement that unfurls as history moves closer to its definitive peak.

As we stand on the incline of disclosure, let us dig further into the pages of Sacred text, directed by a hunger for information and a love for the significant secrets that anticipate our revelation.

KEY LESSONS

Establishes in Hebrew Scriptures Prescience: The idea of the Bliss tracks down its foundations in the Hebrew Scripture, with clues and dreams from prophets like Isaiah and Daniel predicting a heavenly social event of the unwavering prior to looming judgment.

Unequivocal New Confirmation Disclosure: The New Confirmation, especially the letters of the Witness Paul and the Good news of Matthew, gives express insights concerning the Satisfaction. Paul, in his letters to the Thessalonians and Corinthians, divulges the secret, while Jesus Himself in Matthew discusses a partition between the honest and profane.

Emblematic Symbolism in Illustrations: Stories in the New Confirmation, for example, the wheat and the tares and the savvy and stupid virgins, utilize representative symbolism to portray a heavenly arranging and the social occasion of the devoted to a position of security.

Finish in the Book of Disclosure: The Book of Disclosure, created by the Messenger John, offers looks at divine scenes where reclaimed people from each country stand before the lofty position. This symbolism recommends a perfection of the Euphoria, depicting a fantastic get together of the recovered.

Amicable Song in Sacred text: The data accumulated demonstrates that the idea of the Bliss is certainly not a simple religious hypothesis however an amicable tune reverberating through the Sacred writings. It works from Hebrew Scriptures murmurs to unequivocal lessons in the New Confirmation, uncovering a strong story that unfurls as history moves toward its definitive peak.

SELF REFLECTION QUESTIONS

How can we deepen our understanding of the Old Testament prophecies that form the foundation of the Rapture, and what insights might these ancient texts provide for our collective journey of exploration?..
....
....
....
....
....
....
....
....
....
....
....
....
....
....

In considering the explicit revelations in the New Testament, particularly through the letters of Paul and the teachings of Jesus in Matthew, how can we collectively grapple with and apply these insights to our shared understanding of the Rapture and its significance?

As a group, how might we interpret the symbolic imagery present in the parables of the wheat and the tares, as well as the wise and foolish virgins, and what implications do these symbols hold for our collective comprehension of the divine sorting described in relation to the Rapture?

In contemplating the Book of Revelation and its portrayal of redeemed individuals from every nation standing before the throne, how can we collectively discern the culmination of the Rapture and its significance within the broader narrative of End-Times prophecy?

....
....

How do we, as a community of seekers, approach the idea that the concept of the Rapture is not a mere theological speculation but a harmonious melody resonating through the Scriptures? How can we collectively engage with this narrative as it builds from Old Testament whispers to explicit teachings in the New
Testament?...
....
....
....
....
....
....
....
....
....
....
....
....

As we stand on the precipice of revelation together, how can our shared thirst for knowledge and reverence for the profound mysteries inspire us to delve deeper into the pages of Scripture, fostering a collaborative exploration of the divine plan that unfolds as history draws nearer to its ultimate climax?

LIFE CHANGING ACTIVITIES

Aggregate Book of scriptures Review Gatherings: Participate in standard gathering Book of scriptures concentrate on meetings to investigate and examine Old and New Confirmation entries connected with the Delight. This aggregate quest for understanding can cultivate further experiences and shared information.

Sacred text Enlivened Conversations: Sort out bunch conversations that dig into the express disclosures tracked down in the New Confirmation, especially the letters of Paul and the lessons of Jesus in Matthew. These conversations can be a stage for aggregate reflection on the groundbreaking ramifications of Bliss lessons.

Representative Reflection Meetings: Work with intelligent meetings collectively to decipher the emblematic symbolism present in anecdotes like the wheat and the tares and the shrewd and silly virgins. This common investigation can prompt individual and aggregate development in understanding the representative language utilized in scriptural prescience.

Book of Disclosure Investigation: Lead joint examinations zeroed in on the Book of Disclosure, investigating the divine scenes portrayed by the Missionary John. These aggregate investigations can give significant bits of knowledge into the climax of the Delight and its more extensive importance with regards to End-Times prediction.

Local area Love and Consideration: Cultivate a feeling of aggregate love and thought, perceiving the agreeable song of the Happiness story all through Sacred writing. This common profound practice can develop the local area's association with the heavenly arrangement and make an extraordinary encounter for people inside the gathering.

CHAPTER SUMMARY 2: VEILED PROPHECIES

As the sun plunged underneath the skyline, creating long shaded areas across the old city, a feeling of expectation lingered palpably. Teacher Eleanor Faraday remained at the limit of the failed to remember library, a spot supposed to house the keys to unwinding the strange strings of the Bliss.

With a cautious touch, Eleanor followed her fingers along the endured spines of dusty books, every one containing parts of failed to remember predictions and perplexing images. The air was thick with the aroma of old material, as though the actual embodiment of time had been epitomized inside these pages.

Her process had driven her through enigmatic pieces of information and secret entries, yet the responses she looked for stayed slippery. The predictions appeared to move on the edge of cognizance, their implications hidden in layers of allegory and imagery.

As Eleanor dove further into the texts, an example started to arise — an embroidery of occasions woven across hundreds of years. The Satisfaction, it appeared, was not a solitary occasion but rather an intermingling of predeterminations, an inestimable expressive dance coordinated by powers outside human ability to grasp.

In one entry, she revealed a reference to a heavenly arrangement that reflected the plan of stars on a long-failed to remember night. One more indicated a favored one, a figure whose predetermination was interlaced with the destiny of universes.

Eleanor's academic psyche hustled, drawing an obvious conclusion regarding old parchments and current speculations. The strings of the Delight were not straight however entwined, making a perplexing web that spread over the domains of fantasy and reality.

As she translated the texts, a need to get a move on grasped her. The strings were disentangling quicker than she could follow, and the outcomes of this grandiose woven artwork coming unraveled weighed intensely on her shoulders.

With a decided purpose, Eleanor accumulated her discoveries and ready to leave the library. The moon cast an ethereal shine on the city outside, and the night murmured mysteries just the stars could fathom.

Much to her dismay, the strings she unwound were nevertheless a small portion of the enormous plan. The Euphoria's real essence remained covered in secret, its strings prompting places both wondrous and risky. Eleanor's process had recently started, and the unwinding of the strings guaranteed a disclosure that would shape the fate of universes.

KEY LESSONS

Intricacy of Prescience Translation: Unwinding the strings of the Euphoria uncovered the multifaceted and complex nature of deciphering predictions. The data accumulated stressed the requirement for a nuanced comprehension of representation, imagery, and verifiable setting to figure out old messages.

Interconnectedness of Occasions: The assembled information featured the interconnectedness of occasions across existence. The Bliss was not a solitary event but rather a union of fates, underlining the significance of thinking about a more extensive point of view while investigating prophetic stories.

Multidisciplinary Approach: Teacher Eleanor Faraday's process included a multidisciplinary approach, joining bits of knowledge from cosmology, folklore, and old texts. This highlights the benefit of moving toward complex secrets with a different range of abilities, perceiving that answers might lie at the crossing point of various fields of information.

Criticalness in Disentangling Secrets: The need to get a move on felt by Eleanor as she unraveled the predictions fills in as an update that a few secrets might have time-delicate ramifications. Data gathering isn't just a scholarly pursuit however can have certifiable results, inspiring a quick and exhaustive examination.

Impediments of Human Getting it: In spite of Eleanor's academic endeavors, the data assembled alluded to the constraints of human figuring out even with grandiose secrets. The strings of the Satisfaction appeared to escape total perception, underscoring the modesty required while digging into domains that outperform the limits of mortal information.

SELF REFLECTION QUESTIONS

Have we considered the multifaceted nature of prophecy interpretation, recognizing the intricate dance between metaphor, symbolism, and historical context in our quest to understand ancient texts?

In exploring the interconnectedness of events across time and space, are we actively incorporating a broader perspective, understanding that the Rapture is not a standalone event but a convergence of destinies that extends beyond conventional boundaries?

....
....

How well have we embraced a multidisciplinary approach, weaving insights from astronomy, mythology, and ancient texts to create a more comprehensive understanding of the Rapture's threads, acknowledging that answers may lie at the crossroads of diverse fields of knowledge?...
....
....
....
....
....
....
....
....
....
....
....
....
....
....
....
....

....
....

To what extent are we recognizing the urgency embedded in unraveling these mysteries?
....
....
....
....
....
....
....
....
....
....
....
....
....
....
....
....
....

Are we approaching information gathering not only as an intellectual pursuit but also as a practical endeavor with potential real-world

consequences?..
....
....
....
....
....
....
....
....
....
....
....
....
....
....
....
....
....
....

As we delve into cosmic mysteries, have we acknowledged and grappled with the limitations of our collective human understanding?
....
....
....
....
....

....
....
....
....
....
....
....
....
....
....
....
....
....

How does this awareness shape our approach to deciphering prophecies that seem to surpass the boundaries of mortal knowledge?..................................
....
....
....
....
....
....
....
....
....

Are we mindful of the humility required in the face of the unraveling threads of the Rapture, understanding that, despite our collective scholarly efforts, some mysteries may elude complete comprehension?

....
....
....
....
....

How does this recognition influence our ongoing exploration of the cosmic tapestry before us?..
....
....
....
....
....
....
....
....
....
....
....
....
....
....
......

LIFE CHANGING ACTIVITIES

Set out on a Similar Folklore Excursion: Participate in an extraordinary action by digging into relative folklore. Investigate the rich woven artwork of fantasies from different societies to more readily comprehend the interconnectedness of human stories and the all inclusive subjects that might give bits of knowledge into the strings of predetermination.

Stargazing and Heavenly Investigation: Change your life by taking up stargazing and divine investigation. By understanding the galactic references found in old texts, you can fashion a more profound association with the universe, acquiring a point of view that rises above the limits of day to day existence.

Multidisciplinary Learning Undertaking: Set out on a multidisciplinary learning endeavor, separating scholarly storehouses to incorporate information from different fields. By consolidating experiences from space science, folklore, and history, you can develop an all encompassing comprehension that rises above the impediments of a solitary discipline.

Make a Prediction Translating Studio: Start a studio or study bunch zeroed in on disentangling predictions. By cooperatively investigating the complexities of representation and imagery in old messages, members can on the whole unwind secrets and gain a mutual perspective of the grandiose strings that wind through our aggregate predetermination.

Time-Touchy Critical thinking Retreat: Put together a retreat or studio that reproduces time-delicate critical thinking situations. Draw motivation from the criticalness felt by Teacher Eleanor Faraday, underscoring the viable ramifications of unwinding secrets. This movement can develop a feeling of direction and a cooperative soul in moving toward difficulties with a quick and careful mentality.

CHAPTER SUMMARY 3: THE UNVEILING OF ETERNITY

As the last trumpet reverberated through the sky, a heavenly quiet fell upon the Earth. The hotly anticipated second had shown up — the Delight had occurred, and the people who were picked climbed to meet their Maker. Beneath, the world was pushed into disorder, with puzzled spirits wrestling with the unexpected vanishing of friends and family.

In the midst of the natural disturbance, the Incomparable Affliction spread out its dismal wings. Murkiness slipped, both figuratively and in a real sense, as the sun and moon were clouded, projecting the world into a creepy nightfall. It was a period of retribution, a grandiose stage where humankind's deeds were to be investigated.

The scene moved to the sky, where a heavenly court arose — a divine amphitheater where the Sheep of God directed. The Book of Life was opened, uncovering the names of the people who had gotten their place in time everlasting. Holy messengers, clad in brilliant covering, remained as observers to the unfurling show.

The decisions started, every spirit uncovered before the all-knowing look of the All-powerful. Each activity, each rationale, each implicit idea was examined with an accuracy that rose above human cognizance. The balances of equity swung with infinite importance, deciding the timeless destiny of the people.

In the midst of the turmoil, the recovered found comfort in the Sheep's hug, their transgressions washed away by the blood of the symbol of atonement. However, for the people who had picked the way of insubordination, a nerve racking acknowledgment unfurled — the outcomes of their choices scratched across the texture of time everlasting.

The Incomparable Affliction arrived at its crescendo as vast calamities cleared across the globe. Oceans thundered, mountains shuddered, and the actual underpinnings of the Earth shook. It was a visual ensemble of heavenly rage and recovery — a vast expressive dance arranged by the hands of the Maker.

Amidst the turmoil, a last call repeated — a solicitation to contrition and recovery. The Sheep's benevolence broadened even in the last minute, a demonstration of the limitless elegance that rose above the limited limits of human comprehension.

As the Incomparable Hardship faded, another period unfolded — a period past time, where the recovered strolled in the radiance of the Sheep, and the unredeemed confronted the outcomes of their decisions. Forever extended before them, an embroidery woven with the strings of freedom of thought, elegance, and heavenly equity.

Thus, the section of Day of atonement shut, passing on mankind to wrestle with the heaviness of its decisions, as the reverberations of forever resonated across the universe.

Key lesson

Decisions Characterize Time everlasting: The account highlights the significant effect of individual decisions on one's everlasting predetermination. The enormous decisions uncover that each activity, rationale, and believed is shown up the equilibrium, accentuating the significance of careful living.

Beauty In the midst of Judgment: Regardless of the enormous hardships, the story features the persevering through elegance of the Sheep of God. Indeed, even despite divine judgment, there is a call to contrition and reclamation, displaying the vast leniency that continues until the last minute.

Greatness of Time: The idea of forever rises above the fleeting limits of mortal presence. The situation depicted develop past the direct movement of time, stressing the immortal idea of heavenly equity and the never-ending outcomes of human decisions.

The Enormous Ensemble of Reclamation and Rage: The infinite upheavals and heavenly decisions are depicted as an ensemble — an excellent organization of recovery and fury. This symbolism recommends an enormous request and reason behind the turbulent occasions, featuring the heavenly story that unfurls in the embroidery of presence.

The real Job and Penance: The account delivers the topic of confidence and penance, represented by the Sheep of God. The reclaimed track down comfort in the symbol of atonement's hug, underscoring the authentic redemptive force and the significant effect of sacrificial penance on one's timeless predetermination.

SELF REFLECTION QUESTIONS

How have our choices, both seen and unseen, shaped the tapestry of our existence, and are we mindful of the profound impact they may have on our eternal destiny?..
....
....
....
....
....
....
....
....
....
....
....
....
....
....
....
....

In times of cosmic tribulation, do we recognize the enduring grace extended to us, and are we receptive to the call of repentance and redemption, understanding the boundless mercy that persists even in the eleventh hour?

Are we cognizant of the timeless nature of our actions and decisions, understanding that they resonate beyond the linear progression of time, and do we consider the implications of our choices in the broader context of eternity?..
....
....
....
....
....
....
....
....
....
....
....
....
....
....
....
....
....

As we navigate the cosmic symphony of redemption and wrath, do we perceive a greater cosmic order and purpose behind the tumultuous events in our lives, and how does this understanding influence our perspective on divine justice?

Reflecting on the theme of faith and sacrifice symbolized by the Lamb of God, how do we personally relate to the redemptive power of faith, and what sacrifices are we willing to make for a higher purpose that extends beyond our temporal existence?..
....
....
....
....
....
....
....
....
....
....
....
....
....
....
....
....
....
....

In the face of judgment and the consequences of our choices, are we attuned to the cosmic invitation to self-reflection and transformation, recognizing that our journey extends into the vast expanse of eternity, and how does this awareness influence our present actions?..
....
....
....
....
....
....
....
....
....
....
....
....
....
....
....
....
....
....

LIFE CHANGING ACTIVITIES

Mindful Living Practices: Engage in daily practices that foster mindfulness and awareness of our choices. This includes reflection on actions, motives, and thoughts to ensure they align with values that contribute positively to our eternal journey.

Embracing Redemption and Repentance: Actively seek opportunities for personal growth and transformation, recognizing the enduring grace available to us. Embrace a mindset of repentance when necessary, understanding that redemption is a continual process throughout our lives.

Timeless Reflection: Dedicate time to reflect on the timeless nature of our actions. Consider the long-term consequences of decisions, acknowledging that our choices ripple beyond the immediate moment and contribute to the broader narrative of our existence.

Contributing to a Greater Purpose: Align daily actions with a sense of cosmic purpose. View challenges and triumphs as part of a larger cosmic symphony, understanding that our contributions play a role in a grander narrative that extends beyond individual circumstances.

Faith and Sacrifice: Cultivate a deepened sense of faith, recognizing the redemptive power it holds. Additionally, be open to acts of selfless sacrifice for the greater good, understanding that such actions can have profound implications on our spiritual journey and eternal destiny.

CHAPTER SUMMARY 4: EMBRACING HOPE AMIDST CHAOS

As the reverberations of the Satisfaction resound across the world, humankind is left wrestling with a significant vulnerability, an embroidery woven with strings of dread and bewilderment. In this section, we set out on an excursion to explore the obscure, looking for comfort and fashioning a way towards trust and certainty.

The Broke Reality

The prompt result of the Bliss is a scene of broken real factors. Families destroyed, networks left in disorder, and a world wrestling with the unexpected shortfall of endless spirits. The tremendousness of the circumstance can be overpowering, creating a long and overwhelming shaded area over the survivors.

Getting a handle on for Understanding
Despite this phenomenal occasion, looking for understanding is normal. Religious conversations and philosophical discussions might emerge, yet in the midst of the tumult, discovering a feeling of direction becomes principal. People and networks might meet up to share their encounters, endeavoring to get a handle on the baffling.

Local area and Fortitude
As the residue settles, the significance of local area becomes obvious. Manufacture associations with individual survivors; together, you can offer profound help, share assets, and track down strength in solidarity. Whether in petition, shared encounters, or straightforward thoughtful gestures, fortitude turns into a foundation for remaking broke lives.

Rediscovering Confidence

For the people who end up scrutinizing their confidence, the repercussions of the Joy can be an extraordinary period. It is a potential chance to rediscover and rethink convictions, to track down comfort in otherworldliness, and to construct an underpinning of trust that rises above the quick disarray.

Useful Procedures for Endurance

In the functional domain, essential methods for surviving become fundamental. Secure admittance to food, water, and asylum. Lay out correspondence organizations to interface with different survivors and offer data. Flexibility and cleverness become key ethics in the journey for dependability.

Another Typical

As the world changes with another ordinary, flexibility arises as an encouraging sign. Embrace change and track down strength in versatility. The revamping system is an aggregate exertion, and every individual adds to the remaking of a general public that, while perpetually modified, holds the potential for recharging.

End: Exploring the Unknown
Living day to day after the Satisfaction is an odyssey into the obscure, an excursion that requests mental fortitude, strength, and an unfaltering obligation to trust. By embracing the difficulties, tracking down strength in local area, and rediscovering confidence, survivors can explore the strange waters, directing towards a future where trust rules, even notwithstanding the unexplored world.

KEY LESSONS

Local area is Vital: In the outcome of the Euphoria, assembling and keeping up with associations with individual survivors is fundamental. Local area offers profound help, shared assets, and a feeling of solidarity that can assist people with exploring the vulnerabilities of the new reality.

Versatility and Creativity: Reasonable methodologies for endurance incorporate being versatile and clever. From tying down essential necessities to laying out correspondence organizations, the capacity to adjust to the changing conditions and innovatively use accessible assets is critical to strength.

Rediscovering Confidence and Reason: The commotion following the Bliss might lead people to scrutinize their convictions.

Nonetheless, this period likewise offers a potential chance to rediscover and rethink one's confidence, discovering a recharged feeling of direction and trust that rises above the quick mayhem.

Fortitude in Variety: despite misfortune, embracing variety inside the survivor local area becomes urgent. Individuals might have various foundations, convictions, and encounters, however fortitude and acknowledgment cultivate a more grounded aggregate soul, fundamental for modifying broke lives.

Versatility as an Encouraging sign: The excursion into the obscure requires strength. Embracing change, adjusting to new normals, and adding to the aggregate remaking exertion are fundamental parts of a versatile mentality. Indeed, even in a world everlastingly modified,

the potential for recharging and trust stays a
directing light.

SELF REFLECTION QUESTIONS

How can we strengthen our connections with fellow survivors to build a supportive community in the face of uncertainty?..................................
....
....
....
....
....
....
....
....
....
....
....
....
....
....
....
....
....
....

What practical steps can we take to enhance our adaptability and resourcefulness as we navigate the challenges of this new reality together?..
....
....
....
....
....
....
....
....
....
....
....
....
....
....
....
....

In what ways can we collectively explore and rediscover our faith and purpose, finding common ground that uplifts us during these

trying
times?..
....
....
....
....
....
....
....
....
....
....
....
....
....
....
....
....
....

How can we ensure that our survivor community embraces and celebrates the diversity within our ranks, recognizing it as a

source of strength and resilience?..
....
....
....
....
....
....
....
....
....
....
....
....
....
....
....
....
....

As we contribute to the rebuilding process, how can we cultivate a mindset of resilience, embracing change and adapting to the evolving

circumstances around us?..
....
....
....
....
....
....
....
....
....
....
....
....
....
....
....
....
....
......

What shared values and goals can we establish within our survivor community to foster a sense of unity, ensuring that we collectively steer towards a future where hope reigns supreme?

LIFE CHANGING ACTIVITIES

Join or Lay out a Survivor Encouraging group of people:

Draw in with individual survivors to make an encouraging group of people, sharing encounters and assets. This offers close to home help as well as adds to a feeling of local area, essential for exploring the vulnerabilities of life after the Delight.

Basic instincts Preparing Studios:
Put together or partake in studios that attention on functional abilities to survive, underlining flexibility and genius. These exercises can engage people and the local area to deal with moves going from tying down fundamental necessities

to laying out viable correspondence organizations.

Confidence Investigation and Conversation Gatherings:
Work with or join bunches where survivors can straightforwardly investigate and examine their confidence, giving an open door to aggregate rediscovery and redefinition. This encourages a common feeling of direction and trust that rises above the quick turmoil.

Variety and Incorporation Drives:
Find proactive ways to celebrate and embrace the variety inside the survivor local area. Lay out drives that advance getting it, acknowledgment, and solidarity, perceiving the strength that comes from a different gather pursuing a shared objective.

Versatility Building Studios:

Start studios zeroed in on developing strength as an outlook. These exercises can remember conversations for embracing change, adjusting to new normals, and contributing by and large to the reconstructing system. Building a strong local area turns into an extraordinary action that shapes the survivor's point of view toward the post-Delight world.

PART TWO

CHAPTER SUMMARY 5: SIGNS AND PROPHECIES

As we anxiously expect the arrival of Christ, it is foremost to comprehend the signs and predictions anticipating His impending appearance. The Holy book fills in as our compass, giving fundamental data to explore through the intricacies of these times.

1. Scriptural Predictions: Unwinding the Embroidered artwork

Dig into the prophetic sacred writings that have endured everyday hardship. From the book of Daniel to the disclosures in the New Confirmation, these predictions weave an embroidery of occasions prompting Christ's return. Outfit yourself with a careful comprehension of these hallowed stanzas to perceive the unfurling of heavenly plans.

2. Signs On the planet: Deciphering the Times

Inspect your general surroundings for signs that line up with scriptural expectations. Wars, starvations, and catastrophic events are not only occurrences yet rather flags repeating the expressions of Christ. Remain cautious, perceiving the meaning of these occasions as signs of the coming satisfaction of predictions.

3. Profound Readiness: Supporting Your Confidence

While remaining informed is urgent, otherworldly readiness is similarly crucial.

Develop serious areas of strength for an immovable confidence through supplication, reflection, and a profound association with God. As you set up your brain, likewise brace your heart, for an immovable soul will direct you through the vulnerabilities of these times.

4. Local area and Partnership: Strength in Solidarity

Draw in with friends in faith, sharing experiences and supporting each other on this excursion. The people group gives strength and support, encouraging a climate where adherents can all in all get ready for Christ's return. Together, form an organization of confidence that endures the difficulties paving the way to the guaranteed day.

5. Knowing Misleading Lessons: Preparing for Trickery

In a world loaded up with different philosophies, be knowing. Bogus lessons and misdirecting precepts might endeavor to redirect devotees from the genuine way. Arm yourself with information, contrasting all lessons against the perpetual reality of the Sacred texts. An insightful soul is a strong safeguard against double dealing.

6. Watchfulness: Living in Expectation

Christ encouraged us to be careful and prepared. Experience every day with an expectation of His return, keeping a way of life lined up with His lessons. A careful heart keeps you zeroed in on the timeless, cultivating a need to get going in your quest for exemplary nature.

Taking everything into account, as we furnish ourselves with the important data, let us likewise recall the pith of adoration, empathy, and elegance. In getting ready for Christ's return, may our activities mirror the groundbreaking force of His lessons, enlightening the way for us and everyone around us.

KEY LESSONS

Scriptural Establishment: Ground how you might interpret Christ's return in a strong underpinning of scriptural predictions. These immortal sacred texts give the guide, directing devotees through the unfurling occasions prompting His up and coming appearance.

Wisdom and Watchfulness: Foster an insightful soul to explore through the intricacies of various lessons and philosophies. Remain watchful, perceiving the signs on the planet as pointers lining up with the prophetic expressions of Christ.

Profound Readiness: Focus on otherworldly readiness close by gaining information. Develop a profound and steadfast confidence through supplication, reflection, and a solid association with God. A strengthened soul will act as an unflinching anchor despite vulnerabilities.

Local area and Association: Perceive the strength tracked down in local area and partnership. Draw in with faith family, sharing bits of knowledge, and supporting each other. A unified local area gives a wellspring of solidarity and consolation, fundamental for exploring the difficulties paving the way to Christ's return.

Living in Expectation: Embrace a way of life of watchfulness and preparation. Experience every day with a feeling of expectation for Christ's return, adjusting your activities to His lessons. This outlook encourages a consistent quest for uprightness and keeps devotees zeroed in on the timeless point of view.

SELF REFLECTION QUESTIONS

Scriptural Understanding: Have we collectively grounded our knowledge of Christ's return in the Scriptures, ensuring that our understanding is rooted in the timeless prophecies that guide us?

_____
_____
_____
_____
_____
_____
_____
_____
_____
_____
_____
_____
_____
_____
_____
_____
_____

Discernment and Vigilance: Are we collectively developing a discerning spirit, both individually and as a community, to navigate through the complexities of various teachings and ideologies, staying vigilant for the signs that align with Christ's prophetic words?..
....
....
....
....
....
....
....
....
....
....
....
....
....
....
....
....
....

Spiritual Preparedness: How well are we nurturing a deep and unwavering faith as a community? Are we collectively engaging in practices such as prayer, meditation, and maintaining a strong connection with God to fortify our spirits for the uncertainties ahead?

Community and Fellowship: In our collective journey, how effectively are we engaging with fellow believers, sharing insights, and supporting one another?

....
....
....
....
....
....
....
....
....
....
....
....
....
....
....
....
....

Is our sense of community providing the strength and encouragement needed to navigate

the challenges leading up to Christ's return?..
....
....
....
....
....
....
....
....
....
....
....
....
....
....
....
....

Living in Anticipation: As a collective, are we fostering a lifestyle of watchfulness and readiness? How are our shared actions reflecting an anticipation for Christ's return, and are we collectively aligning our lives with His

teachings?..
....
....
....
....
....
....
....
....
....
....
....
....
....
....
....
....
....

Guarding Against Deception: How well are we, as a community, guarding against false teachings and misleading doctrines? Are we collectively using our discernment to compare all teachings against the unchanging truth of the Scriptures?

LIFE CHANGING ACTIVITIES

Sacred writing Submersion Retreats: Arrange and take part in vivid retreats zeroed in on diving into scriptural predictions. These retreats can act as extraordinary encounters, extending how you might interpret Christ's return and giving a common space to aggregate learning and reflection.

Wisdom Studios: Host studios inside your local area to foster insight abilities all in all. These meetings can incorporate reasonable activities, conversations on recent developments considering scriptural lessons, and cooperative endeavors to fortify the local area's capacity to perceive truth from duplicity.

Profound Development Gatherings: Lay out little gatherings inside your local area devoted to otherworldly arrangement. These gatherings can take part in ordinary petition, reflection, and study meetings, cultivating an aggregate obligation to building and strengthening every part's confidence.

Local area Effort Drives: Expand your local area's solidarity and backing to the more extensive society through outreach drives. This mirrors the lessons of Christ as well as enhances the feeling of cooperation, having an unmistakable effect on the existences of those out of luck.

Expectant Way of life Difficulties: Energize and challenge each other to live with a ceaseless feeling of expectation for Christ's return. This could include laying out aggregate objectives lined up with His lessons, encouraging a way of life of thoughtfulness, empathy, and preparation for the timeless point of view.

CHAPTER SUMMARY 6: THE LIFELINE OF LOVE

Amidst vulnerability, where shadows of uncertainty pose a potential threat, there exists a convincing way to deal with share the immortal message of Jesus — a help reached out to the people who might feel abandoned in the rhythmic movement of life's difficulties.

Embracing Sympathy
Fundamental to this approach is the unflinching hug of empathy. To successfully convey the lessons of Jesus, we should initially grasp the battles and vulnerabilities that others face. It is through veritable compassion that we produce an association, making a scaffold for the groundbreaking force of affection and confidence to navigate.

Fitting the Message
Perceiving the different embroidery of human encounters, our methodology should be nuanced and versatile. One size doesn't fit all with regards to sharing the message of Jesus. Fitting our correspondence to reverberate with the interesting excursions of the people who might feel left behind permits the message to puncture through the commotion of vulnerability and arrive at the profundities of the spirit.

Meeting Them Where They Are
In the advanced age, the life saver should reach out into the virtual domains where individuals look for comfort and replies. Using on the web stages, virtual entertainment, and sight and sound assets becomes basic in arriving at the people who might be actually far off yet

sincerely present. By meeting them where they are, we show a promise to separating obstructions and building associations.

Thoughtful gestures as Declarations
Talk is cheap, and thoughtful gestures become strong declarations to the extraordinary love of Jesus. Participating in beneficent deeds and local area administration tends to quick necessities as well as fills in as an unmistakable articulation of the standards Jesus educated. These activities become encouraging signs, drawing others toward the wellspring of that empathy.

Making Comprehensive People group
In dubious times, the help of confidence is braced through the obligations of local area. Making comprehensive spaces where people from varying backgrounds can share their questions, fears, and goals cultivates a climate

where the message of Jesus isn't recently spoken however resided. Such people group become living declarations to the persevering through force of adoration and acknowledgment.

Supporting Profound Mentorship
Perceiving the significance of direction, profound mentorship assumes a crucial part in this methodology. Offering a strong hand to the individuals who might be grappling with vulnerability gives a life saver that steadies them on their profound excursion. Mentorship goes past doctrinal lessons; it turns into a customized guide, enlightening the way toward a more profound comprehension of the message of Jesus.

All in all, the help to the people who might feel abandoned in dubious times is woven with strings of sympathy, versatility, inclusivity, and activity. By encapsulating the lessons of Jesus in our cooperations, we expand a help that salvages as well as enables people to explore the turbulent oceans of existence with unflinching confidence and love.

KEY LESSONS

Sympathy as an Establishment: The significance of sympathy is a common subject, underscoring the need to move toward others with compassion and understanding, perceiving their interesting battles and vulnerabilities.

Versatility in Correspondence: Recognizing the different encounters of people, the methodology highlights the need of fitting the message of Jesus to reverberate with the changed excursions individuals embrace, guaranteeing a more significant and important association.

Advanced Commitment for Effort: In the cutting edge age, expanding the help includes using on the web stages and computerized apparatuses to contact people who might be actually far off yet sincerely present. This features the significance of meeting individuals where they are, even in the virtual domain.

Talk is cheap: Exhibiting the lessons of Jesus through unmistakable thoughtful gestures and local area administration turns into a strong declaration. Activities address prompt requirements as well as act as noticeable articulations of the groundbreaking force of affection and confidence.

Building Comprehensive People group: The making of comprehensive spaces and networks is significant. These conditions, portrayed by acknowledgment and variety, give a sustaining scenery to people to investigate and embrace the message of Jesus. Inclusivity turns into a foundation for cultivating further associations and understanding.

SELF REFLECTION QUESTIONS

How well are we embodying compassion in our interactions with others, and in what ways can we deepen our understanding of their unique struggles and uncertainties?

In reaching out to diverse individuals, how effectively are we adapting our communication to resonate with the varied journeys and experiences that make up our community?

Are we leveraging digital platforms to the fullest extent, ensuring that we are meeting people where they are, even in the virtual realm? How can we enhance our online outreach efforts?..
....
....
....
....
....
....
....
....
....
....
....
....
....
....
....
....

In our collective actions, how are we exemplifying the teachings of Jesus through acts

of kindness and community service? Are there opportunities to amplify our impact and make these actions more visible within our community?..
....
....
....
....
....
....
....
....
....
....
....
....
....
....
....
....
....

To what extent are we succeeding in creating inclusive spaces and communities that reflect the acceptance and diversity inherent in the teachings of Jesus?

....
....
....
....
....
....
....
....
....
....
....
....
....
....
....
....

How can we strengthen these environments to foster deeper connections among individuals of different backgrounds?..................................
....
....
....

....
....
....
....
....
....
....
....
....
....
....
....
....
....

As a collective, how well are we nurturing spiritual mentorship within our community?
....
....
....
....
....
....
....
....
....
....

....
....
....
....
....
....
....

Are there ways we can enhance our support systems to guide individuals on their spiritual journey and provide a steadying hand during times of uncertainty?..
....
....
....
....
....
....
....
....
....
....
....
....
....

LIFE changing activities

Set out on a Sympathy Excursion: Take part in exercises that develop compassion and empathy, for example, chipping in local area administration projects or taking an interest in outreach programs. Effectively look for chances to comprehend and reduce the battles of others.

Embrace Versatile Correspondence Practices: Change your correspondence style by deliberately fitting your message to resound with the different encounters of everyone around you. Go to studios or courses zeroed in on compelling correspondence and social aversion to upgrade your versatility.

Advanced Effort Drives: Saddle the force of innovation for positive change. Start or effectively take part in web-based gatherings, conversation gatherings, or online entertainment crusades that bring the message of trust and confidence to people who might be actually far off yet carefully present.

Thoughtful gestures Challenge: Genuinely promise to routinely perform purposeful thoughtful gestures. Whether it's aiding a neighbor, supporting a nearby foundation, or partaking in local area drives, let your activities be an unmistakable articulation of the adoration and empathy exemplified by the lessons of Jesus.

Develop Comprehensive People group: Play an influential position in encouraging inclusivity inside your local area. Coordinate occasions that celebrate variety, empower exchange among people of various foundations, and effectively pursue establishing a climate where everybody feels acknowledged and esteemed.

These extraordinary exercises line up with the standards talked about as well as engage people to experience the groundbreaking message of Jesus in their day to day routines effectively.

CHAPTER SUMMARY 7: NAVIGATING THE END-TIMES MAZE

Question 1: How might we recognize indications of the Final days?

In the midst of vulnerability, many look for signs to decipher the unfurling of the Last days. Sacred text encourages us to be cautious, noticing the signs like conflicts, catastrophic events, and moral rot. However, it's memorable's vital that main God knows the specific timing (Matthew 24:36). Rather than focusing on signs, center around developing an unwavering and exemplary life.

Question 2: What is the job of adherents during the Last days?

Devotees are called to stand firm in their confidence, sharing the Gospel and offering desire to people around them. Sacred writing urges us to be salt and light in a world confronting difficulties (Matthew 5:13-16). Trust in God's sway and effectively partake in His redemptive arrangement.

Question 3: Will there be a one-world government or a worldwide request referenced in the Good book?

While the Good book doesn't expressly specify a one-world government, it suggests when a worldwide authority might arise. Center around developing acumen and remain established in the lessons of Christ. Know about common powers yet place extreme confidence in God's command over all countries (Daniel 2:21).

Question 4: How could we get ready for the Final days?

Planning includes otherworldly availability more than actual arrangements. Consistently take part in supplication, concentrate on Sacred text, and fortify your relationship with God. Develop a heart of sympathy, pardoning, and love, for these excellencies will support you in testing times (Matthew 22:37-39).

Question 5: Is the possibility of the Joy upheld by Sacred text?

The idea of the Joy, however not expressly referenced, is gotten from refrains that talk about devotees being up to speed to meet Christ. Translations might shift, however the substance lies in the confirmation of gathering with the Ruler. Center around carrying on with a day to day existence satisfying to Him as opposed to becoming involved with discusses (1 Thessalonians 4:16-18).

Question 6: How would we explore dread and tension about the Final days?

Dread not, for God is with you (Isaiah 41:10). Recognize that dread is normal yet divert it towards confidence. Ground yourself in the commitments of God and the timeless expectation tracked down in Christ. Look for help from faith family and support each other in the midst of pain (Philippians 4:6-7).

Question 7: What is the meaning of the hardship time frame?

The hardship is a time of extreme testing and decontamination. While its precise nature is discussed, the center message is clear: stay loyal in the midst of preliminaries. Believe that God's equity will win, and His leniency will support His kin (Disclosure 7:14).

All in all, as we explore the labyrinth of End-Times situations, let us focus on Christ, the creator, and perfecter of our confidence (Jews 12:2). Look for His direction through petition and drench yourself in His Promise for the insight expected to explore these unsure times.

KEY LESSONS

Carefulness without obsession: While it's critical to know about signs demonstrating the Last days, try not to focus on unambiguous occasions or timetables. Trust in God's amazing luck, as just He knows the exact unfurling of these occasions.

Dynamic support in God's arrangement: Devotees assume a vital part during the Final days. As opposed to capitulating to fear, effectively partake in God's redemptive arrangement by sharing the Gospel, being a wellspring of trust, and experiencing a dedicated and honest life.

Profound planning over actual arrangements: Spotlight on otherworldly preparation through supplication, Sacred writing study, and building areas of strength for a with God. While a few down to earth arrangements might be shrewd, the accentuation ought to be on developing ethics that support the soul in testing times.

Solidarity in variety of convictions: Perceive that understandings of End-Times situations might differ among devotees. Rather than getting caught in discusses, focus on solidarity in the center lessons of Christ. Underscore love, sympathy, and pardoning as binding together excellencies.

Confidence over dread: Dread is a characteristic reaction to vulnerability, however divert it towards confidence. Ground yourself in God's commitments, look for help from faith family, and encourage a mentality of trust and trust.

Recall that God is in charge, and His ideal love projects out dread.

SELF REFLECTION QUESTIONS

How well are we balancing vigilance and fixation in our understanding of End-Times signs? Are we trusting in God's timing or becoming overly preoccupied with specific events?...
....
....
....
....
....
....
....
....
....
....
....
....
....
....
....

**In what ways are we actively participating in God's redemptive plan during these uncertain times? How can we collectively be a source of hope and share the Gospel with those around us?..
....
....
....
....
....
....
....
....
....
....
....
....
....
....
....
....
....
......

**Are we prioritizing spiritual preparation over physical provisions in our lives?

....
....
....
....
....
....
....
....
....
....
....
....
....
....
....
....
....

How can we collectively strengthen our spiritual resilience through prayer, Scripture study, and building a stronger relationship with God?...
....
....

**How do we navigate unity within our diverse beliefs about End-Times scenarios?

Are we fostering a spirit of love, compassion, and forgiveness, recognizing the common ground we share in the core teachings of Christ?

....
....
....

**In the face of uncertainty, how are we collectively redirecting fear towards faith?
....
....
....
....
....
....
....
....
....
....
....
....
....
....
....
....

Are we consistently grounding ourselves in God's promises, seeking support from fellow believers, and fostering a mindset of trust and hope?

....
....
....
....
....
....
....
....
....
....
....
....
....
....
....
....
....

**Reflecting on our understanding of the End-Times, how well are we embodying the virtues of faith, love, and compassion in our interactions with others?

....
....

How can we collectively grow in these virtues to better navigate the challenges that may arise?

LIFE CHANGING ACTIVITIES

Day to day Profound Everyday practice: Lay out an extraordinary schedule that incorporates day to day supplication and committed time for concentrating on Sacred writing. This predictable practice will fortify your otherworldly establishment, giving direction and versatility notwithstanding vulnerability.

Local area Commitment: Connect effectively in your neighborhood local area or church. Be a wellspring of expectation and backing for other people, sharing the Gospel through your activities and empowering a feeling of solidarity. This contribution can carry reason and satisfaction to your life.

Careful Reflection on Dread and Confidence: Foster an extraordinary propensity for careful reflection when overcome with dread. Delay to divert dread towards confidence, establishing yourself in God's commitments. This propensity will enable you to confront difficulties with a quiet and confiding in soul.

Uprightness Development Challenge: Start an individual or gathering challenge zeroed in on developing excellencies like love, empathy, and pardoning. Routinely survey your advancement and celebrate development, cultivating an extraordinary climate that emphatically influences your life and everyone around you.

Worldwide Mindfulness and Petitioning God Organization: Make or join a request network that rises above geological limits. Remain informed about worldwide occasions, particularly those lining up with potential End-Times situations. Commit time to aggregate petition for the world's prosperity, developing a feeling of interconnectedness and reason in your life.

PART THREE

CHAPTER SUMMARY 8: FINDING SOLACE IN SCRIPTURE

Amidst life's tempests, a directing light rises up out of the immortal insight of sacred writing. These refrains act as mainstays of solidarity, offering a safe house of solace when the world feels overpowering. We should investigate an assortment that resounds with the pith of flexibility.

1. Song 23:4 - The Shepherd's Affirmation
"Despite the fact that I stroll through the haziest valley, I will fear no malicious, for you are with me; your pole and your staff, they solace me."

In the shadows of misfortune, the symbolism of God as a consoling shepherd gives comfort, guaranteeing us that we are in good company.

2. Isaiah 41:10 - Dread Not, For I'm With You
"So don't fear, for I'm with you; don't be overwhelmed, for I'm your God. I will fortify you and help you; I will maintain you with my noble right hand."

A steadfast commitment that rises above time, this section ingrains fortitude by stressing the heavenly presence during attempting times.

3. Philippians 4:13 - Strength in Christ
"I can do everything through Christ who fortifies me."

This section fills in as a strong update that our solidarity isn't self-produced; rather, it streams from a higher source, engaging us to confront any test.

4. Matthew 11:28-30 - Tracking down Rest in Christ
"Come to me, all you who are fatigued and troubled, and I will give you rest. Take my burden upon you and gain from me, for I'm delicate and humble in heart, and you will track down rest for your spirits."

In the midst of life's disarray, this section welcomes us to track down comfort in Christ, promising a helpful harmony for the tired soul.

5. 2 Corinthians 1:3-4 - Divine force of All Solace
"Acclaim be to the God and Father of our Master Jesus Christ, the Dad of empathy and the Lord of all solace, who solaces us in the

entirety of our difficulties, so we can comfort those in any issue with the solace we, at the end of the day, get from God."

This sacred writing stresses the repeating idea of solace, featuring that our own battles become a wellspring of sympathy for other people.

As we explore the rhythmic movement of life, these refrains stand as immortal anchors, giving strength and solace that rises above the difficulties of our excursion. In snapshots of sadness, let these words be a shelter, a safe-haven of unfaltering help grounded in the timeless realities of sacred text.

KEY LESSONS

Divine Presence in Adversity:

Song 23:4 and Isaiah 41:10 underline the soothing presence of a higher power during testing times, encouraging a feeling of confirmation and fortitude.

Enabled Through Confidence:

Philippians 4:13 instructs that strength comes through Christ, empowering a mentality of dependence on trust to defeat hardships.

Supportive Harmony in Christ:

Matthew 11:28-30 welcomes people to track down rest and comfort in Christ, depicting Him as a wellspring of revival for the exhausted soul.

Recurrent Nature of Solace:

2 Corinthians 1:3-4 features the correspondence of solace, proposing that the comfort got during preliminaries turns into a wellspring of sympathy and backing for others out of luck. Ageless Insight as Anchors:

The sacred writings act as immortal anchors, giving getting through strength and solace that rises above the transient difficulties of life, offering a solid starting point for exploring the intricacies of the human excursion.

SELF REFLECTION QUESTIONS

How can we actively cultivate a sense of divine presence in our lives, drawing inspiration from Psalm 23:4 and Isaiah 41:10, especially during moments of adversity?

In what ways can we strengthen our faith and reliance on Christ, as suggested by Philippians 4:13, to navigate challenges collectively and find empowerment as a community?..
....
....
....
....
....
....
....
....
....
....
....
....
....
....
....
....
....
....

As we face weariness and burdens in our lives, how can we collectively embrace the invitation

from Matthew 11:28-30 to find rest in Christ, ensuring that our community becomes a source of rejuvenation for each other?..
....
....
....
....
....
....
....
....
....
....
....
....
....
....
....
....
....

Considering the cyclical nature of comfort highlighted in 2 Corinthians 1:3-4, how can we actively contribute to creating a supportive

community where the comfort we receive becomes a source of empathy and solace for others?..
....
....
....
....
....
....
....
....
....
....
....
....
....
....
....
....
....
....

How can we integrate the timeless wisdom of these scripture verses into our collective mindset, recognizing them as anchors that provide enduring strength for our community

amid life's challenges?..
....
....
....
....
....
....
....
....
....
....
....
....
....
....
....

In what ways can we, as a community, ensure that the lessons derived from these scriptures become guiding principles, shaping our interactions and responses to collectively foster resilience and comfort within our shared

journey?..
....
....
....
....
....
....
....
....
....
....
....
....
....
....
....
....
....
....
....

LIFE CHANGING ACTIVITIES

Laying out an Everyday Otherworldly Practice:

Carrying out a day to day schedule that incorporates snapshots of supplication, reflection, or contemplation to encourage a feeling of heavenly presence, drawing motivation from Hymn 23:4 and Isaiah 41:10.

Local area Strengthening Studios:

Facilitating studios or social events zeroed in on building aggregate confidence and dependence on Christ, roused by Philippians 4:13, to enable people inside the local area to confront difficulties with a versatile mentality.

Local area Rest and Recharging Occasions:

Sorting out occasions or exercises that give a space to aggregate rest and revival, lining up with the standards of Matthew 11:28-30, where local area individuals can find comfort and backing from each other.
Encouraging groups of people and Guiding Administrations:

Laying out local area encouraging groups of people and guiding administrations in light of the standards of 2 Corinthians 1:3-4, perceiving the significance of common solace and sympathy in the difficult situation.
Coordination of Sacred writing in Local area Values:

Implanting the ageless insight of the sacred texts into the fundamental beliefs of the local area, guaranteeing that the examples got from these stanzas become core values for aggregate connections and reactions, encouraging versatility and solace inside the local area's common process.

CHAPTER SUMMARY 9: NAVIGATING RELATIONSHIPS IN A TRANSFORMED WORLD

In this post-Happiness period, where the structure holding the system together has gone through a significant change, the immortal insight of scriptural lessons fills in as an undaunted aide for exploring the complexities of our connections.

1. Empathy in Turmoil:

In the midst of the vulnerability and disturbance, embracing the uprightness of sympathy becomes principal. Drawing from scriptural standards, let us recollect the expressions of Colossians 3:12 - "In this manner, as God's picked individuals, blessed and profoundly cherished, dress yourselves with sympathy, consideration, modesty, tenderness, and tolerance." In a world reshaped by heavenly occasions, our connections ought to be established on understanding and compassion.

2. Absolution as Freedom:

In a domain where remainders of the past might torment us, pardoning arises as a freeing force. Matthew 6:14 confers, "For in the event that you pardon others when they sin against you, your glorious Dad will likewise excuse you." In a post-Euphoria world, the capacity to pardon turns into a strong method for mending broke connections, encouraging solidarity, and preparing for aggregate reclamation.

3. Local area Building:

The idea of local area is enhanced in a world that has encountered a heavenly shift. Acts 2:44-45 represents the early Christian people group, expressing, "Every one of the adherents were together and shared everything for all intents and purpose. They offered property and assets to provide for any individual who had need." In a comparative soul, the post-Joy world requires a feeling of collective obligation, where we share assets, support each other, and construct strong bonds.

4. Acumen in Choices:

The changed scene requests elevated acumen in direction. Sayings 3:5-6 exhorts, "Entrust in the Master with everything that is in you and lean not on your own comprehension; in the entirety of your ways submit to him, and he will make your ways straight." This rule stays important as we explore new difficulties, underscoring dependence on divine direction for good instinct in a world reshaped by heavenly powers.

5. Love Past Limits:

The decree to cherish each other takes on a significant importance in a post-Happiness reality. 1 Corinthians 16:14 reminds us, "Do everything in adoration." Love turns into a binding together power that rises above natural limits, cultivating concordance and participation among different people exploring a changed world.

As we wrestle with the intricacies of connections in a post-Bliss world, mooring ourselves in these scriptural standards gives an immortal establishment to cultivating sympathy, pardoning, local area, wisdom, and love. In applying these lessons, we track down pragmatic direction for exploring the complicated embroidered artwork of our relational associations in this new period.

KEY LESSONS

Sympathy as a Core value:
Embrace sympathy, generosity, lowliness, tenderness, and persistence as fundamental components in connections, drawing motivation from Colossians 3:12. In a post-Joy world, exploring intricacies with an empathetic outlook encourages understanding and sympathy.

Pardoning as a Freeing Power:
Perceive the force of pardoning, repeating the lessons of Matthew 6:14. In a changed world, relinquishing past complaints becomes fundamental for individual freedom, mending cracked connections, and adding to aggregate recovery.

Local area Driven Living:

Construct a feeling of local area likened to the early Christian model in Acts 2:44-45. Sharing assets, supporting each other, and developing mutual obligation reinforce bonds in a post-Bliss world, encouraging flexibility and solidarity.

Acumen in Direction:

Apply elevated acumen in direction, heeding the guidance from Sayings 3:5-6. Trust in divine direction for savvy instinct, perceiving the requirement for a resolute anchor in a world reshaped by heavenly occasions.

Love Rising above Limits:

Focus on affection as an all-encompassing rule, roused by 1 Corinthians 16:14. In a world changed, love turns into a binding together power that rises above natural limits, adding to

concordance and participation among different people exploring the intricacies of the post-Euphoria reality.
Compassion Checkpoint:

How well would we say we are encapsulating the characteristics of empathy, thoughtfulness, lowliness, tenderness, and tolerance in our associations with others, particularly in this post-Joy world?
Pardoning Assessment:

In thinking about our connections, would we say we are effectively captivating in the freeing demonstration of absolution, perceiving its extraordinary power as accentuated in Matthew 6:14?
Local area Association Evaluation:

How can we add to the feeling of local area, drawing motivation from the Demonstrations 2:44-45 model, and what steps could we at any point take to additional upgrade public bonds in our changed reality?
Wisdom in Direction:

Is it safe to say that we are reliably looking for divine direction, as prompted in Axioms 3:5-6, to educate our choices in the face regarding the one of a kind difficulties introduced by the post-Euphoria world?
Love Past Limits Reflection:

In our day to day cooperations, how are we typifying the rule of getting along everything in adoration, as taught by 1 Corinthians 16:14, and in what ways could we at any point grow this affection to rise above natural limits?
In general Otherworldly Development Request:

Considering the illustrations drawn from scriptural lessons, how can our aggregate otherworldly development advance because of the intricacies of the post-Euphoria world, and what changes could we at any point make to adjust all the more intimately with these immortal standards?

Sympathy Challenge:

Take part in really difficult where every day includes deliberately rehearsing sympathy, thoughtfulness, modesty, delicacy, or persistence. Ponder how this deliberate center changes your connections and connections. Absolution Custom:

Start a pardoning custom, whether through an individual diary or verbal articulations, where you intentionally discharge any waiting complaints. Permit the freeing force of pardoning, motivated by Matthew 6:14, to bring a reestablished feeling of opportunity and harmony.

Local area Building Occasion:

Sort out a local area building occasion propelled by the Demonstrations 2:44-45 model. This could include a common dinner, cooperative undertakings, or an asset sharing drive, cultivating a more grounded feeling of solidarity and backing inside your local area.

Wisdom Retreat:

Commit an end of the week to an insight retreat, detaching from the typical interruptions. Mull over Precepts 3:5-6, looking for divine direction and lucidity on significant choices. Utilize this intelligent opportunity to acquire experiences that illuminate your way ahead.

Love-in real life Challenge:

Send off an affection in real life challenge where, motivated by 1 Corinthians 16:14, you purposefully complete day to day demonstrations of adoration past your standard circles. Archive the effect of spreading love, rising above limits, and cultivating agreement in different associations.

SELF REFLECTION QUESTIONS

Compassion Checkpoint:
How well would we say we are exemplifying the characteristics of sympathy, graciousness, lowliness, tenderness, and tolerance in our cooperations with others, particularly in this post-Joy world?..
....
....
....
....
....
....
....
....
....
....
....
....
....
....
....

Absolution Assessment:

In pondering our connections, would we say we are effectively captivating in the freeing demonstration of absolution, perceiving its extraordinary power as underlined in Matthew 6:14?

Local area Association Evaluation:

How can we add to the feeling of local area, drawing motivation from the Demonstrations 2:44-45 model, and what steps could we at any point take to additional improve common bonds in our changed reality?..
....
....
....
....
....
....
....
....
....
....
....
....
....
....
....
....
....

Wisdom in Navigation:

Might it be said that we are reliably looking for divine direction, as exhorted in Precepts 3:5-6, to educate our choices in the face regarding the special difficulties introduced by the post-Satisfaction world?..

Love Past Limits Reflection:

In our day to day cooperations, how are we epitomizing the guideline of getting along everything in adoration, as trained by 1 Corinthians 16:14, and in what ways could we at any point grow this affection to rise above natural limits?..
....
....
....
....
....
....
....
....
....
....
....
....
....
....
....

By and large Profound Development Request:

Considering the illustrations drawn from scriptural lessons, how can our aggregate profound development advance because of the intricacies of the post-Joy world, and what changes could we at any point make to adjust all the more intimately with these ageless standards?

LIFE CHANGING ACTIVITIES

Compassion Challenge:

Take part in really difficult where every day includes deliberately rehearsing empathy, graciousness, modesty, tenderness, or persistence. Ponder how this deliberate center changes connections and connections inside your local area.

Pardoning Custom:

Start a pardoning custom, whether through mutual social events or shared rehearses, where members deliberately discharge any waiting complaints. Permit the freeing force of pardoning, propelled by Matthew 6:14, to bring a reestablished feeling of opportunity and harmony to the system.

Local area Building Occasion:

Sort out a local area building occasion enlivened by the Demonstrations 2:44-45 model. This could include a common feast, cooperative undertakings, or an asset sharing drive, encouraging a more grounded feeling of solidarity and backing inside the local area.
Insight Retreat:

Plan an insight retreat for the local area, giving an open door to aggregate reflection and contemplation on Maxims 3:5-6. Urge members to look for divine direction and clearness on significant choices, encouraging a common feeling of direction and course.
Love-in real life Challenge:

Send off an adoration in real life challenge for the whole local area where deliberate demonstrations of affection past recognizable circles are empowered everyday. Record the effect of spreading love, rising above limits, and encouraging concordance in assorted collaborations all through the local area.

Made in the USA
Las Vegas, NV
20 April 2025